Self-Defense Survival!

Keeping yourself safe in everyday street situations

By

Nigel Taylor

Introduction

This book is not intended to tell you what moves to do if you are attacked this way, or attacked that way. It simply doesn't work like that, because in reality you simply won't know what you would do until it happens, hopefully it won't so you never have to find out. This book is designed hopefully to help make you think more clearly about the potentially dangerous areas and situations that you might be placing yourself in, after all, prevention is better than the cure, in other words you only fight as a last resort, the key to all this is not to find yourself in that situation in the first place if at all possible.

So what is self-defense? Learning self-defense should not be about teaching you how to "Go the distance" in a street fight or how to "Teach someone a lesson" and above all most certainly is not about being a bully or attacking others when unprovoked.

You are learning valuable survival skills, what to do in case you are attacked, how to gain that momentary edge over your attacker so you can get away or find people who can help you.

There's a huge difference between self-defense and fighting! If you are attacked your number one priority above all should be to get away as quickly and as safely as possible, your goal is not to try to win a fight but escape unhurt. Of course in order to escape you may need to disorient, distract, stun, and even disable your attacker. But once you see an opportunity to escape, take it and get out of there, don't hang around and admire your handy work.

Areas covered in this book

1) Be aware of your surroundings
2) Different types of confrontations
3) How much force can I use?
4) Staying safe without fighting
5) Striking vulnerable areas

Chapter 1
Be aware of your surroundings

Don't be distracted by cell phones, stay focused as someone could be following you!

Prevention is the best defense, by avoiding certain situations you can minimize your risk of being attacked, such as scanning your environment for suspicious activity and being alert at all times instead of just blindly walking around. Avoid dangerous areas like poorly lit and isolated places, late at night in unfamiliar territory, and stay away from people who might be prone to violence such as drunks or gangs.

Unfortunately, even if you are street smart, there are too many incidents of random, unprovoked violence nowadays. If someone attacks you, your life may be in danger. You must react quickly and confidently. The longer you wait, the harder it may become to free yourself. There is no time for social graces, or being polite and reserved, you must respond as the situation requires. Anything goes! After all, an attacker is not coming for your autograph! Do whatever is necessary to gain an advantage and get out of there quickly.

Many assaults and robberies are done by opportunists. They are not specifically out to get you yourself, but rather someone, anyone. Walking around the streets talking on a cell phone, listening to music through headphones and openly showing off expensive jewelry can be huge distractions and dangers that could make you the next victim of an opportunist. Do not make yourself vulnerable in this manner.

If you must go walking around at night if it's at all possible plan out exactly where you are going and walk there confidently looking like you know where you are, do not slowly walk around looking lost like some kind of mesmerized tourist looking at everything in sight. This will simply put you right on top of an opportunists list to be robbed or assaulted.

Many dangerous situations can be avoided by using common sense. For example, park your vehicle somewhere that does not offer concealment to a potential attacker to lie in wait for your return especially if it's after dark, think about what you're doing, don't make it easy for them.

Surprise attacks can be very difficult to deal with especially if you are distracted by the above things we just mentioned and not concentrating. Not only could you be taken out with the first blow it's also very difficult to get into a combative mind set while you are hurt and in shock over actually being assaulted. But for someone who is well trained in self-defense it's easy to immediately switch on the aggression and deal with the situation you now find yourself in, after all, this is the reason you went to self-defense training in the first place right? It's not all about learning something for a hobby, you may have to use these skills one day!

One carefully aimed and controlled punch is way more effective than flailing wildly with your head down like some kind of out-of-control-windmill or something just hoping you might get lucky and hit your attacker. The chances are you won't succeed.

So, it's better not to be caught by surprise if at all possible. Staying in lit public places will give you a better chance of staying safe. Even then, you must still be on your guard at all times.

Deceptive attackers often use distraction techniques such as asking you for the time or for a cigarette. This gives them the opportunity to get in close enough to you in order to launch their attack without warning. If at all possible do not let a stranger get within arm's reach. Once inside that area you could be in serious danger.

If you find yourself in this position and are feeling uneasy with this stranger do not just stand there, to any passersby you will look like two people having a conversation and they won't know what's really happening. Stepping back with your arms raised will send the alarm bells ringing alerting passersby you need help. If you follow these

5 steps you will have a better chance of staying safe and getting help.

1) If you are feeling uneasy about this stranger approaching you put your hands up, this is a sign that says you are not interested.

2) If you really sense you are in danger shout at your attacker before he gets too close "Back off!" he may suddenly run away at this point. This will also give passersby notice that you might be in an uncomfortable situation leading to a confrontation and may need their help.

3) It's possible no passersby may be visible and if he is still coming towards you it's now time to scream and shout loudly! This will hopefully make him run and also alert people, after all, even if they can't see you they can hear you and come to your rescue.

4) When all else has failed it's time to defend yourself. With your hands raised to protect against punches or grabs, step back on your strongest leg, you are now in a position to deliver a very strong kick if need be.

5) If you managed to stun your attacker, you may possibly have only have a few seconds before he recovers and comes at you again, do not stand there admiring your handy work, get away as fast as possible! You have been given a chance to survive, take it and run!

Now, having said all that, until you actually do get attacked you cannot possibly know what you would do, you can only imagine what you might do and with the adrenalin flowing like crazy your actions might not be exactly what you had hoped, but I can guarantee you will do one of the following 3 things…

1) Freeze and get attacked and possibly injured!

2) Fight back!

3) Turn and run away!

The last option would be the safest of the 3 options ensuring no harm comes to you, the first option is by far the worst thing to do as you are going to get attacked for sure in one way or another. The second option is very risky as again you risk being injured, you can only hope your attacker would run away because you took him by surprise by fighting back. But like I said, you won't know for sure until it actually happens, we can only hope you never have to find out.

It would be impossible to make yourself completely attack proof, but you can make yourself be an undesirable target, not by acting tough and aggressive as these actions can trigger an attack, but there are a few measures you can take that will make a potential attacker overlook you and search for an easier target instead by staying focused and looking alert, remember if you're the type that's wandering around in a world of your own listening to music you are making yourself a very easy target to sneak up on, by the time you realize what's happened it could be too late.

How a potential attacker sees your posture and demeanor are two highly important things that could dictate whether you get attacked or not, a slouched looking down at the ground kind of posture makes you a much easier target than someone who is upright, alert and businesslike.

Basically, if you appear to be confident and comfortable in your surroundings you are much less likely to be an attacker's next victim. Try to always think before potentially putting yourself in danger that way you might avoid any unwanted confrontations and fights. Remember, when it comes to your safety prevention is always better than the cure.

A good everyday self-defense tool to carry around-especially for the ladies-is a ball point pen, while it seems like a very innocent looking item it can be easily concealed and it really can be used to great effect by placing your thumb over the top and jabbing your attacker anywhere you can hit! It will deliver a very painful blow and could easily get you out of a very dangerous situation.

Chapter 2
Different types of confrontations

A person's body language can often give warning and prepare you for a possible confrontation!

Confrontations even between friends can suddenly erupt over petty things, basically a different opinion over something can easily trigger this and if alcohol is involved things could get out of hand pretty quickly.

The key is to not allow yourself to get drawn into this type of situation by remaining calm and by never putting yourself directly in front of someone who is clearly acting in an aggressive manner and looking for a confrontation. Keep your distance and hopefully the situation will be defused quickly.

The usual pattern of behavior for this situation to start is by an exchange of words which can become insulting and threatening, nearly always accompanied by arm waving and gesturing and even throwing objects that might be within reach before coming to physical blows.

Here's the three main types of confrontations you may have seen or experienced yourself at some time, all are pretty common.

1) An individual who is gesturing for you to "have a go" from a distance is usually a sign his bark is worse than his bite, in other words he's more of an exhibitionist rather than a fighter. Unless you say something that really hits a nerve making him suddenly attack you he'll probably just be satisfied with a barrage of insults then head off to tell his friends how he won a fight that never even happened! A frustrating situation, but a far better outcome however than an actual fight. Words can hurt for sure, but so can getting beaten senseless.

2) Occasionally a confrontation can really escalate, when someone not only talks bad but actually gets closer to you and starts pushing and grabbing then this is a very serious threat indeed. Once this has reached that point it will keep escalating till you either do something to make him back off or an outside intervention ends the situation, but at this point simply hoping for the best is not going to help you at all, the talking stage is well and truly over and it's now time for action!

3) You might find yourself in a confrontation with someone who skips all the above and goes straight into violence against you. At this point anything goes as you have no idea how far your attacker may take things, he may be satisfied with hitting you a couple of times, but equally he may be satisfied with knocking you down and kicking you in the head while you are helpless on the ground. Passersby may decide to join in and help you, then again they may completely ignore the situation, it can and does happen. The point is once this has reached the physical level you have no way to know just how bad it might get, your life may be in danger at this point.

So, to recap here are briefly the three main types of confrontations we just talked about…

1) Someone who is all talk and has little intention of actually fighting, you are unlikely to be at too much risk from this type of individual apart from being called a few bad names.

2) Someone who takes the confrontation to the next level by pushing and grabbing. You are at possible risk from this type of individual unless you protect yourself from the possible attack that is very close to happening.

3) Someone who goes straight into the violence without any kind of warning, you are at most risk from this type of individual. You have no time to be on your guard here as you are at severe risk from an unprovoked attack, the surprise of which can result in serious injury.

Most of the people that like to start fights really have no idea how to fight in the first place! Many are nothing more than bullies picking a fight with someone who doesn't stand much chance of beating them relying on aggression and intimidation which can work in their favor simply because untrained people don't know how to handle those two things and are basically beaten before a punch is thrown.

Although anything can happen in a fight there's a definite trend to what actually does happen, the buildup, such as the posturing and threats is very common as is the grabbing and pushing. Once the fighting actually starts you'll nearly always see the big overhead swinging punch with the stronger hand from the person throwing it proving they know nothing about fighting at all! Also wrestling on the ground is another favorite it seems. Real fights are certainly nowhere near as exciting or interesting as the ones you see in the Kung-Fu movies, but of course they are not real.

Don't react like a victim. How you react to a potential confrontation is very important. There is nothing wrong with being polite and considerate as long as you make it very clear that you are choosing to be civil rather than being coerced by the aggressor. It is possible to head off many potentially serious problems by taking a stand early on and making it clear that you have no intentions of accepting the situation that could develop.

Deterrence. This stand can take one of two forms, which are best described as deterrence and de-escalation. Deterrence is quite a bold response, even though it doesn't have to be aggressive or rude, basically you're making a bold statement saying enough is enough! The only problem with this being if you're not a match physically for the potential attacker it could be like waving a red flag to a bull leading to an escalation of the situation.

De-Escalation. This is just the opposite approach, you are trying to appeal to his good nature, assuming he has one that is. Instead of making a bold response you try to calm things down or make an excuse for why you are backing off, this might mean you are apologizing for something you haven't even done in the first place! But if it ends the possible threat then take that to be a victory. De-Escalation can be a good strategy as it allows the potential attacker to go on his way believing he made you stand down in fear of him. However, many confrontations are fueled by nothing more than over inflated egos so this strategy could backfire on you by pushing him down onto a position in which his ego forces him to attack you. Think wisely before using either of these two strategies.

During a confrontation always make sure you know where your potential attacker's hands are at all times, while you can see them the biggest threat is receiving a punch but when their hands disappear under clothes there's a good chance they will produce a weapon such as a knife. If this happens don't wait to see what they surprise you with! The moment their hand goes under clothing act fast! Lunge forward jamming their arm against their body while delivering a barrage of strikes with your other hand. A knife threat will be much easier to deal with while it's still concealed under clothing, but once drawn and out in the open the danger level has been significantly increased.

If you are facing an attacker who has you at gun point, you are in a whole new level of danger! No matter how good you are at martial arts you aren't going to dodge a bullet! It's not like in the movies where the hero avoids the bullets with his lightning fast reflexes, try this in the real world and you will be seriously injured or killed in seconds!

If you are facing someone at gunpoint then you are most likely about to be robbed. Whatever possessions the attacker wants give them up immediately! Remember, your attacker doesn't have to be close to you for you to be hurt with a gun.

Bottom line is this, your life is seriously on the line! No matter how valuable items may be for the most part they can be replaced. Your life however, cannot!

Chapter 3
How much force can I use?

A good example of a restraining hold is a head lock shown in this pic on a dummy.

If you do find yourself in a situation where you must defend yourself how much force is acceptable to use in order to get the better of your attacker?

You have the right to protect yourself or someone else from violence by using force but your actions should be appropriate to the level of threat you find yourself dealing with, in other words, don't go over the top after you have dealt with your attacker.

If you have to hit someone 50 times to stop them attacking you this is acceptable providing they were still a threat after punch number 49! But if you continue to punch or kick them after they are helpless on the ground then the table has been turned around and now you are the aggressor and can be prosecuted as such.

Now, having said that, this doesn't mean you have to wait till you are punched first before using force to stop your attacker, if you wait till you are punched before taking action the first punch could well be the last punch too!

Anyone can be taken out with one punch so don't wait, act fast!

You are entitled to use an appropriate level of force as soon as you recognize a threat to yourself. Notice I say `appropriate` and not `minimum` force? This is because the law does not require a person to carefully figure out exactly what level of force is required to stop an attack or use a specific move to stop the danger, so providing your actions are reasonable under the circumstances you are quite within your rights to do what is needed but no more than that. Remember don't get carried away and turn yourself into the aggressor.

The level of force used must be appropriate to the threat that you perceive it to be and you have to be able to justify your perception. Hitting someone who isn't a threat but in your eyes looks a `bit dodgy` is not acceptable at all. But if you can explain exactly what signs of aggression you felt threatened by and feared for your safety, then as long as your response was proportionate to the threat you feared, then your actions are justified by law.

Once the threat is over you must stop as further violence is not necessary and certainly no longer self-defense at all. You are entitled to ensure your attacker is unable to continue, but certain guidelines apply here, it's acceptable by using a restraining move but most certainly not acceptable by kicking them on the ground. Control is the key here.

There is no `he came at me with a knife so I killed him` principle, but if your only course of action to stop an attacker from doing something extremely serious to you resulted in his death or very serious injury, then as long as you actions were warranted by the circumstances, they would be considered lawful.

You are not required by law to try to escape from a situation or to surrender any more than you are to stand and fight. However, if do claim self-defense then you will need to explain why you chose this option rather than using other means not using force. For example, if you chose to stand and fight someone when you had a clear chance of escape, you would be required to explain why you did not take that opportunity. If there wasn't a good reason for your choice of action, then this might undermine your assertion that you only did what you had to do in order to protect yourself.

If you have the attitude that the person deserved a `good kicking` for attacking you in the first place you have taken this way past self-defense as self-defense only applies while there is a threat. It's amazing how quickly your attacker will happily play the role of victim and sue you should you step over the line for something they started in the first place!

So basically, if you decide you want to get some `payback` after the threat is over you will most likely answer for it in a court of law, remember, there are cameras on most streets now watching your every move that will confirm whether your actions were justified or not. Again, control is the key here, I cannot stress that enough.

Chapter 4
Staying safe without fighting

Showing a passive gesture may defuse the situation and possibly avoid an unwanted confrontation.

The whole idea behind self-defense is not to see your attacker as an enemy that must be destroyed, but rather the goal is to ensure your own safety and get away from any potential dangerous situation. That may well mean fighting to achieve this, but, there are other ways that can work just as well.

There is nothing cowardly about avoiding a fight if at all possible, actually it makes sense to avoid unnecessary conflict. After all, you cannot get hurt or injured from a fight that never happened, but many times peoples egos will get in the way of this and they'll see avoiding a fight as a sign of weakness and because of this they'll fight when they don't have to and possibly get injured.

I'm sure you'll remember your dear old mom telling you as a young kid about not talking to strangers, getting in cars with strangers and walking down dark alleys alone, yet so many people forget this kind of advice years later and put themselves in unnecessary danger.

Many victims of assaults say afterwards that they saw it coming, so the problem is not being able to spot the danger they have put themselves in, but rather, unable to act on it once they see it coming. The thinking of `that kind of thing happens to other people, not me` is a very dangerous attitude to have.

The lack of common sense in avoiding these potentially dangerous situations is very evident by the choices people make. For example, Friday or Saturday after the bars close can be a huge area of concern, fast food joints is where you'll see many fights, the drunks are out in force and many looking for trouble!

Poorly lit or lonely areas are very hazardous at night, some are well known and some even have a bad reputation, but yet people will blindly ignore these red flags if it means getting home a few minutes early by walking down a dark lane as a short cut, many times fueled by alcohol their brains are telling them "it'll be ok, no problem just this once" and it might be ok just this once, but you can definitely reduce your risk of danger by avoiding these areas. Just a little thought can save you a lot of trouble.

Quite often, you might encounter a gang of teenagers hanging out on the street corner at night who are doing just that and don't intend anyone any harm, but if you feel uneasy about walking past them then don't, seek another route to take. It is very easy to tell if someone could be trouble by their demeanor and attitude, if your instincts are warning you it's for a good reason, don't hang around if you feel threatened, if it's at all possible to leave before any confrontation can happen, then it's best to do exactly that. Always be scanning your horizon for possible dangers. Think ahead, be one step ahead of any possible danger.

If someone is approaching you looking for trouble for whatever purpose, you cannot always predict what the potential attacker is looking for, but one thing you can be sure of is this-it's not a fight they're looking for, they are not expecting you to fight back because they are simply looking for a victim who they believe would be easy prey. If you happen to be of small build then you could have a problem.

Even the aggressors who just want to hit someone for no good reason are looking to get their joy at minimal cost to themselves, if you appear confident they will most likely see you as a bigger threat to them than they are to you and move on to the next person hoping they will provide an easier target. Similar actions to that of a bully who we know are nothing more than cowards.

Now, one of the interesting things of knowing self-defense is simply no one can tell what you're capable of doing just by simply looking at your size, an aggressor is highly unlikely to try and assault a bodybuilder because of the sheer size of the person and the aggressor would naturally assume him to be stronger than he is even though a bodybuilder might not know how to fight, he's a huge visual deterrent. As we already said he's nothing more than a bully so wouldn't think of attacking someone bigger and stronger than himself, but a martial arts expert can come in any shape imaginable which can be to your advantage or not depending on the potential attacker's perspective of you.

One of my favorite stories regarding this matter was when my old sensei was walking back to his car with groceries one night, the guy was in his late 50`s, little over 5 feet tall with a beer belly! Sounds like an easy target right? That's what three thugs thought as they jumped him, what they didn't know was… he was a 9th degree black belt in Japanese Ju-Jitsu! Three thugs went to hospital very quickly! My old sensei said he had a bit of fun with them which involved various punches, kicks, choke holds and throws then called an ambulance for them and took off leaving them feeling very sorry for themselves groaning on the ground. Lesson learned the hard way! Just because someone is smaller and outnumbered doesn't mean they will play the part of the victim. Now, this was an extreme case in that not too many people would possess the expertise, courage and confidence to take on three people bigger than themselves and defeat them with ease.

The one thing you must never allow to happen under any circumstances is for an aggressor to take you elsewhere. Do not allow yourself to be driven away anywhere! Your chances of survival just took a massive blow if you are now in the aggressor's choice of location and you can be sure whatever he has in store for you is seriously bad.

Chapter 5
Striking vulnerable areas

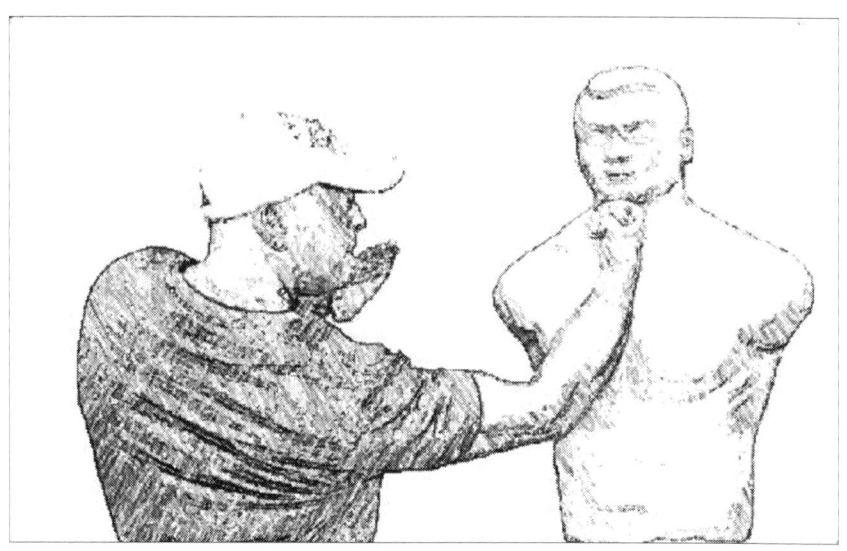

One carefully aimed strike against a vulnerable area is way more effective than wildly lashing out and hoping to hit your target.

Remember, if you are attacked your priority is to ensure your safety, getting an aggressor to let go of you does not end the situation. Many people have been hurt because they didn't take strong enough measures allowing the attacker to have another go at them, you might not get so lucky second time around so don't hold back, you might only get one chance to escape the situation.

One strike could save you from further danger and give you your best chance to end the situation, so hit hard and hit fast! You don't have to wait till your attacker punches you before you think of striking them. Once you deliver that first blow do not stand back and see what your attacker decides to do next, keep on going until the threat is dealt with. Remember, while there is still a threat to your safety it is still self-defense and you must do whatever it takes to ensure your safety. Do not hold back with your first strike, make it count.

You should never reach full extension of your arm before hitting a target with a punch. Many times you will see someone throw a punch with just enough power to reach the intended target almost like they're afraid of hurting their hand so pull the punch short, the secret is to image your target behind the actual target you are striking ensuring maximum force when delivered, that way your strike is actually still accelerating as it goes into the target area rather than slowing down.

Here`s a few of the most vulnerable areas on the human body, if you can strike out at any of these areas you will have a great chance of surviving any attack you might be facing.

Eyes... Striking the eyes is a great way to escape from an attacker who is much stronger than yourself who has managed to get in close enough to grab you and has you in a bear hug. The technique should see your first two fingers spread and bent slightly ensuring you don't break your own fingers if you happen to miss the target and strike your attackers forehead instead. Simply push your hand forward and upwards to your attacker's eyes, aiming a little lower with your fingers sliding up the cheeks into the eye socket is far better than aiming too high. This move will definitely make someone back off a few seconds if not longer stunning them, but don't rely on this to end the situation, be prepared to follow it up with something else immediately then make your escape.

Groin... Kicking the groin if timed and aimed correctly can stop an attacker dead in his tracks. It can be a great way to keep your attacker at a distance before he gets in too close to you. However, if you attempt this kick from a distance be aware that if the distance is too far you might not generate enough power to stop your attacker and only land your kick with the tip of your toes should you even strike the desired target. You are putting yourself in a position of being very off balance as your kicking leg is so extended making it very easy to miss and kick the stomach or leg instead allowing your attacker the chance to grab your leg and push you onto the ground, so don't gamble everything on this one kick, be prepared to follow it up immediately. But if you do manage to time your kick with the distance perfectly this will end any threat you are under. No matter how big and strong someone is a kick to the groin will disable anyone long enough to ensure your escape and safety.

Throat... Punching, chopping and squeezing the throat can stop an attacker immediately. Two of the main strikes are the web hand and the straight fingered strike, both are delivered with a hard straight jabbing action. The web hand strike uses the `L` shape between the thumb and forefinger as a striking surface. The other common throat striking method is to ram straight stiff fingers into the throat. Action against this particular area can be effectively carried out from a close in range or from a distance as very little pressure is needed to make an attacker back off.

However, something to be mindful of is striking with too much force in this area could easily kill someone, so unless your life is in serious danger be very careful when attacking the throat.

Ears... Attacking the ears is a great way to get yourself out of danger, especially if you should find yourself in some kind of close grab or bear hug type of situation where you simply don't have enough space to generate any kind of effective strike. Striking the ears in a clapping motion will definitely disorientate your attacker giving you valuable seconds in which to make your escape to safety.

Shins... The shins have a large number of nerve endings close to the surface of the skin and as such can be a very painful area to receive a kick. Also, the inner side of your foot can be used to slide down an attackers shin. Both the impact and pain caused by this action could well be enough to cause your attacker to lose his balance a few seconds and step back. If you happen to be wearing hard shoes then kicking with your toes will be very effective. If you are grabbed from behind striking the shins is a great area to hit.

Fingers... The fingers offer a great target and are very useful when it comes to getting an attacker to release you from any hold they may have you in. The beauty of this area is the fact there's so many of them and pulling, twisting, bending or even breaking a finger can be extremely painful. Any of these actions should help give you the opportunity to escape.

Nose... The nose is a very delicate area and a solid strike against it can seriously knock the fight out of someone very quickly, it's amazing how someone-even an attacker-can panic when they feel their own blood running out of their nose and into their mouth, the sensation and taste of which can really unsettle someone. A punch, chop or palm-strike are very effective on this particular area whether it be from a distance or close in. Definitely one of the best areas to attack.

Remember, when attacking these or any other areas with your self-defense moves don't make the mistake of stepping back and waiting to see what reactions your attacker is showing after you took action, you might only get one chance at surviving the attack so get out of there immediately!

Meet the author

Nigel Taylor is originally from Chesterfield, a small market town in the county of Derbyshire, which is in the north of England. He exchanged the rain and cold weather of his homeland for the sunshine and heat of south Texas back in 2001 where he's lived ever since and operates his own successful personal training business specializing in kick boxing and self-defense based out of Round Rock Texas, where he now lives with his beautiful wife Stormy and crazy dog Charlie Taylor who resembles Scooby Doo and Zola Taylor a beautiful retired young greyhound. Oh, and not forgetting Snickers too, she's also very much part of this happy dog-loving family who just happen to have their own series of dog adventure books too.

Made in the USA
San Bernardino, CA
29 October 2018